Table of Contents

Introduction

Chapter 1 — Life Coaching: A Fast Rising Global Industry

Chapter 2 — The Different Types of Life Coaching Services

Chapter 3 — What Do Life Coaches Do?

Chapter 4 — How Do Life Coaches Deliver Their Services?

Chapter 5 — The Coaching Process

Chapter 6 — How Much Money Can You Make As A Life Coach?

Chapter 7 — Can You Become A Life Coach Right Now?

Chapter 8 — Preparing to be a Life Coach (Part 1)

Chapter 9 — Preparing to be a Life Coach (Part 2)

Chapter 10 — Trial And Error Can Doom Your Life Coach Career

ProsperWithWayne.com

Chapter 11　　　The Key To Life Coach Success: Proper Accreditation

Chapter 12　　　Getting The Word Out About Your Life Coaching Practice

Conclusion

BECOME A SIX-FIGURE LIFE COACH

DISCOVER HOW YOU CAN BE A CERTIFIED LIFE COACH

WAYNE SUTTON

ProsperWithWayne.com

Become a Six-Figure Life Coach

Discover How You Can Be a Six-Figure Life Coach

Wayne Sutton
® Copyright 2016

ProsperWithWayne.com

© **Copyright 2016 - All rights reserved.**

This document is geared towards providing exact and reliable information in regards to the topic and issue covered. The publication is sold with the idea that the publisher is not required to render accounting, officially permitted, or otherwise, qualified services. If advice is necessary, legal or professional, a practiced individual in the profession should be ordered.

- From a Declaration of Principles which was accepted and approved equally by a Committee of the American Bar Association and a Committee of Publishers and Associations.

In no way is it legal to reproduce, duplicate, or transmit any part of this document by either electronic means or in printed format. Recording of this publication is strictly prohibited and any storage of this document is not allowed unless with written permission from the publisher. All rights reserved.

The information provided herein is stated to be truthful and consistent, in that any liability, in terms of inattention or otherwise, by any usage or abuse of any policies, processes, or directions contained within is the solitary and utter responsibility of the recipient reader. Under no circumstances will any legal responsibility or blame be held against the publisher for any reparation, damages, or monetary loss due to the information herein, either directly or indirectly.

Respective authors own all copyrights not held by the

ProsperWithWayne.com

publisher.

The information herein is offered for informational purposes solely, and is universal as so. The presentation of the information is without a contract or any type of guarantee assurance.

The trademarks that are used are without any consent, and the publication of the trademark is without permission or backing by the trademark owner. All trademarks and brands within this book are for clarifying purposes only and are the owned by the owners themselves, not affiliated with this document.

ProsperWithWayne.com

Introduction

Everyone has life lessons they can share with others. I'm sure you don't need me to remind you of that. You should already know that. If you are a person who has some level of self-awareness as well as empathy, you know this well. Life is full of lessons.

Whether we're going through good times or bad times, life is sure to teach us a thing or two. These life lessons apply across the board. Whether we're talking about our relationships, our career, personal success or even personal productivity, you are bound to pick up a lesson or two as you live your life. Unless you are a hermit stuck on top of a mountain somewhere, any kind of social interaction is bound to give you some important lesson regarding the human experience.

On top of all of this, it's important to note that as we live our lives, we tend to figure out certain "hacks." These are small lessons that we learned that would enable us to do things faster, cut corners, save time, be more efficient, or save money. Whatever the case may be, through trial and error, we learn many different lessons as we go through life. These lessons are important to us. It helps us get more things done, it helps us to pack a lot more value in the things that we do, and it enables us to relate to other people better.

As important as these hacks may be to us, they're equally as important to other people. Interestingly enough, we usually don't share these hacks. In most cases, we only tell our family and friends. Indeed, unless we are asked, we don't even share this information with those closest to us. We tend to keep these small personal life lessons in a small, tight social circle. In fact, a lot of us simply keep these life lessons to ourselves. This really is too bad because you could be making a tremendous amount of money with those "hacks" you've discovered by simply living your life.

I know this is hard to believe considering that you think that these hacks apply only to certain parts of your life. You might be thinking that these are just small fixes that you came up with along the way, but what if I told you **that you can make money teaching these life lessons to others as a life coach?**

That's right.

By teaching these hacks to people who are looking to gain a competitive edge, figure out a new approach to an old problem, or simply looking for new information, you can make quite a bit of money.

Just how much money is there to be made in life coaching?

Well, let's put it this way, according to Ibis World Business Research, the life coaching industry is blowing up in the United States and elsewhere. It is a fast growing industry. According to latest estimates, the annual sales of this industry have passed $800 million. In fact, it is expected to breach the $1 billion mark soon enough.

Get this, **the average life coach hourly rate is $214 per hour.**

ProsperWithWayne.com

Put simply, there's a lot to be made in simply sharing the little life lessons you've learned along the way. Get on this train while it's still early because the moment it becomes institutionalized, you will face stiff competition. This competition usually tends to drive down hourly rates. This happened in other industries and it's bound to happen in the life coaching industry in the United States and elsewhere. However, there is a solution to that as well... we'll discuss that later.

This book teaches you what you need to do to get started with life coaching. It also clues you in on one particularly powerful source of competitive advantage you need to adopt as soon as possible.

As you are read this book and find yourself ready to discover more on how you can become a six-figure life coach within just a few weeks from now – go to http://www.ProsperWithWayne.com and check it out!

Chapter 1

Life Coaching: A Fast Rising Global Industry

According to Ibis World Business Research, the global life coaching industry is just under $800 million and is projected to generate sales of $1 billion or more in a relatively short period of time. This industry is still experiencing red hot growth trends. It's not slowing down any time soon. According to industry forecasts, the life coaching industry will continue to remain red hot, as far as growth and global sales figures are concerned, for years to come.

Why is There a Rising Demand for Life Coaching?

If you pay attention to what happened to the US and global economy after the great financial crash of 2008, it's very easy to see why life coaching is as hot as it is. In the wake of the great recession, more and more people started experimenting with alternative careers. Prior to 2008, the typical life cycle of a middle class person in the United States was that this person went to college, worked for a few years in the corporate world, then went to graduate school, and then worked at an executive job or some mid-level management job. This was the typical life cycle of a middle class American, and the great recession of 2008 destroyed that.

There was no more certainty regarding a straight career progression from point a to point b. Also, thanks to the internet, mobile commuting or remote commuting has redefined the modern workplace. Put these two factors together and you have a massive distributed base of highly talented people with very important skills to share.

On the demand side, a lot of consumers woke up to very fragmented or granular coaching needs. For example, if somebody needed coaching regarding their fashion accessories or parallel choices, thanks to the life coaching market, that person can get expert assistance. Similarly, somebody looking for a job can get career coaching assistance from somebody with extensive job search success history.

Thanks to the rise of mobile devices, making the internet almost ubiquitous, our "always connected" society is more ready, willing and able to tap into individualized pools of expertise without expecting to go through some sort of formal institutional channels. You don't have to go into a brick and mortar building just to get targeted coaching regarding an issue in your life that you are having trouble with. You only need to get online and talk with somebody over Skype, and pay that person for his or her time via PayPal.

ProsperWithWayne.com

This hyper-fragmented micro transaction, multi-interest marketplace is very dynamic and consumers' expectations have really changed over a relatively short period of time. Make no mistake about it, a lot of the frustrations, anxieties and stresses individuals in the United States and in the western hemisphere, as well as western Europe, feel are still there. What's changed is the range of acceptable sources of assistance.

It used to be that if you're having trouble with your career choices or you're feeling a lot of stress in your life, you would go to somebody who has a formal title, who works in a building, and you have to go through some sort of bureaucratic structure.

Not anymore.

Consumers' mindsets have changed regarding how compartmentalized and granular their needs are and they are very open to using the internet to get access to specialized niche counseling.

Will These Trends Persist?

If you're getting excited about becoming a life coach or enjoining this fast growing industry, it's understandable that the next question that would enter your mind is one of durability.

Will these trends persist?

ProsperWithWayne.com

Is there going to be a market by the time you get established in your life coach practice?

This is a perfectly valid question to ask and I'm happy to report that **the answer is a resounding yes**.

The change in consumer mindset regarding the granularity of the need for specialty niche advice is not going to go any time soon. As people become more accustomed to interacting with the broader world through their mobile device like a smartphone or a tablet, the need for such hyper segmented advice is not just going to persist, but it's going to grow.

You have to understand that when you look at a person's needs, it can actually be broken down into finer and finer points of distinction. For example, if somebody is having trouble looking for a job, that person can get counseling regarding confidence building, makeup and general appearance, apparel and wardrobe coaching, speaking skills, and so on down the line.

People are looking for niche specialties that tackle their issues with rifle shots instead of going with a generalist image consultant to take a shotgun approach to their range of issues. By specializing as well as keeping your eyes on the broad trends of your niche, you can stay several steps ahead of market developments to ensure that your coaching skills and specialized body of knowledge will remain in demand for a long time to come.

Go on over to http://www.ProsperWithWayne.com to discover how you can become a professional life coach within just a few weeks!

Chapter 2

The Different Types of Life Coaching Services

To try to categorize life coaching services into neat little boxes is going to be a very frustrating task. It's like trying to capture the rainbow. It's just not going to happen because, as I've mentioned in Chapter 1, there are so many specialized sub-niches and "specialties within specialties" that you really run the risk of painting with too broad of a brush or simply overlooking key points of distinction. With that said, life coaching services do tend to break down into a few fairly readily identifiable niche categories. Again, take this with a grain of salt because I am in no way pretending that this is going to be an exhaustive list.

Career Coaching

Career coaching generally involves advising people how to find job opportunities, apply for such jobs properly, adequately prepare for the interview and prepare for their first day on the job. It also involves how to deal with rejection. Beyond that broad framework, however, there are subsidiary specialty coaching segments like wardrobe selection, confidence training, resume writing and so on down the line.

What these specialized coaching niches have in common is that they tend to focus around career counseling as a shared point of reference. The end objective here is fairly straightforward. It's all about getting the right job and getting the most out of your career until you move on to the next stage of your career development.

Dating Coaching

Another big sub-segment of the life coaching service industry are coaches who specialize in meeting members of the opposite sex. While the demand for this type of service is fairly easy to understand among men, interestingly enough, a lot of women are also requiring dating coaching.

Dating coaching typically focuses on self confidence, presentation, finding the technical aspects of finding a date offline and online, and conversation skills training. A key part of this part of this training focuses on what you should do before, during and after the date. A lot of it also works with you to help you overcome the fear of rejection and how to deal with rejection in a positive way.

Personal Success

Personal success is a broader umbrella category that actually "bleeds into" a wide number of life coaching sub-niches. Personal success tips impact your career choices, your business decisions, and of course, your love life. It is a fairly broad framework that focuses on key skills that actually have a wide range of applications.

This should not be a surprise because learning how to be confident on a personal level can impact how you identify and work with business opportunities. It also can play a big role in how you approach members of the opposite sex and deal with romantic rejection. As far as career goes, confidence is extremely important, it goes without saying. Still, despite the commonalities, personal success life coaching has a lot more to do with establishing the right mindset. As the old saying goes, if you fail to believe, you're not going to achieve.

Personal success, in a thumbnail, is all about reprogramming negative mental habits that produce the same failed results so you can achieve better results. In short, if you want to start experiencing different results, you have to start doing things differently, this goes without saying. But the problem is, for people to start behaving differently, they have to start thinking differently.

ProsperWithWayne.com

Our attitudes and mindsets are manifested in how we act. Personal success is all about destroying negative mental habits and displacing them with a personal attitude framework and mindset that has a higher likelihood of leading to better actions and decisions, which in turn lead to greater personal success overall.

Productivity Coaching

Productivity coaching is a very tightly defined sub-niche of life coaching. Its area of coverage is the precise opposite of personal success. While personal success may tend to paint with a broad brush and cover a fairly large territory, productivity coaching is very narrow. It's all about maximizing your time.

The animating idea behind productivity coaching is to maximize the value that you get for every minute of your time you invest in any kind of activity. You try to squeeze as much money and results for every minute of time you invest in a particular activity.

Among the different coaching sub-niches, productivity coaching pay the most attention to "hacks." These are small incremental changes that add up to dramatic improvements in return on investment, return on effort, and accrued value of time.

It's easy to think of productivity coaching as joined at the hip, so to speak, with career coaching. That would be underestimating this life coaching sub-niche. In fact, productivity coaching's key lessons can be applied to almost all areas of your life.

Since its focus is on maximizing the amount of value for every unit of time you invest, it can be applied to meeting members of the opposite sex. It can also be applied to your relationships. Indeed, it can bring real meaning into, and turn into reality, the often repeated phrase of "quality time."

Business Coaching

Business coaching is a life coaching sub-niche that focuses primarily on identifying business opportunities, taking steps to properly take advantage of business opportunities and running business to maximize profit. Other areas explored by this life coaching sub-niche involve networking, financial resource management, and other core business topics.

The animating principle behind business specific life coaching is return on investment, return on effort, and productivity. It also focuses on maximizing opportunities. It can be very broad that's why there's a lot of internal segments within this sub-niche of the life coaching industry. Within the greater business coaching ecosystem are coaching service providers focused on start-ups, others focus on raising funds, while others are focused on smoothing over potential conflicts between business partners.

Alternative Life Coaching

This major sub-niche of the larger life coaching service category defies easy categorization. It's all over the place.

It's kind of like a catchall category for any type of coaching that doesn't neatly fit into the major categories I described above. It can run the gamut from horoscope or astrology based life coaching, to religious or spirituality-based life coaching, to prepper coaching.

What these coaching sub-segments have in common is that they either draw their inspiration from unusual bodies of knowledge or they use unorthodox means to solve a particular personal hurdle. In the discussion below, I'm only going to cover two of the biggest segments of alternative life coaching: religious coaching and prepper coaching.

Religious Coaching

Religious coaching draws on the moral and philosophical principles of established religions. Whether we're talking about Christianity, Buddhism, Hinduism, or Islam, or other religions.
Whether somebody is trying to overcome fear, get over pride, bounce back from a defeat, and other issues, many people will turn to religious coaching.

ProsperWithWayne.com

I am a minister of the Christian faith, and thus I often find myself in the realm of religious coaching.

Whether you are starting a new phase in your life, trying to take things to the next level, or leaving an old phase behind, religious coaching can provide very powerful advice. This advice is scripture based. It's not like the life coach is just pulling stuff out of the thin blue air. There is some scriptural grounding to the advice they give.

This is extremely important because whenever we talk about scripture, regardless of religious source, we are tapping into hundreds, if not thousands of years of recorded human experience. These are very important lessons learned in many different parts of history, in different cultural contexts, that are united in their universal application to the human condition regardless of space and time.

If anything, what makes religious coaching so powerful is that they often focus on helping the individual push past the boundaries of selfishness and self-limitation. By tapping into the power of the infinite, we get one step closer to some sort of cosmic consciousness that not only ties us with the rest of sentient beings on the planet, but we are also given the power to dig for the answers deep within.

Prepper Coaching

A fast growing sub-segment of the alternative life coaching market space is prepper coaching. Preppers are individuals who are preparing for a future catastrophe.

Whether that catastrophe takes the form of a nuclear attack, a tsunami, a massive earthquake, or multiple volcanoes blowing up all over the world, leading to a new ice age, Preppers seek to be prepared. They are looking for coaching on what food to stock, how to set up a panic room or a survival bunker, as well as practical tips on surviving when "the grid" goes down.

As modern human beings, we are all part of the grid. It's very hard to imagine life without electricity and running water. Preppers understand how dependent we are on these modern amenities and that's why there's a huge demand for topic specific coaching on how to not just survive, but thrive when "the grid" falls apart.

What if there was a massive earthquake right now and there is no electricity, no power, no water? How can you purify water? How can you find water in the first place? How can you generate your own alternative sources of power? These, as well as emergency training tactics are taught by life coaches who specialize in the prepper market segment.

Go on over to http://www.ProsperWithWayne.com to discover how you can become a professional life coach within just a few weeks!

Chapter 3

What Do Life Coaches Do?

Now that you have a clear idea of how big the life coaching market is, and the major segments within this market, the next question in your mind is, what exactly do life coaches do? Since you're thinking of becoming a life coach yourself, it's important to have a clear idea of what exactly you would be doing.

There are no black and white lines separating a specific task categories. However, looking at all the different things life coaches could possibly do and advise on, they tend to fall into five different task areas.

Again, this is just for illustration purposes. Depending on the specific life coach you train with, they might have more tasks and categories, or less. Just keep this in mind because these illustrate the fairly broad areas of services you would provide your clients.

Identifying Client Issues

These tasks focus on working with the client to put their finger on what issues they need to solve. In many cases, clients would come to you and tell you that they're facing certain challenges. It turns out that after a few questions, they have a bigger challenge they're grappling with.

For example, it may turn out that somebody comes to you looking for career coaching, but actually be looking for confidence training. This person has such a profound lack of self confidence and extremely low self esteem that they can't seem to move on in many different areas of their life. While their biggest challenge is getting and keeping a job, that's just the tip of the iceberg.

Identifying client issues is a really important group of tasks because it requires you to read people.

You can't just rely on what people tell you they need.

You need to be able to read between the lines.

You need to be able to connect the dots and get to the bottom of the issue.

It may seem like the problem is fairly superficial and technical in nature, but it may turn out that it's actually connected to something deeper, more profound, and personally significant to them.

By helping them work through those deeper issues, you might be able to assist them in taking their lives to the next level across the board. For example, going back to the scenario of the person with a job issue, by helping that person with his low self confidence, you may be able to help him with his dating life, romantic life, quality of friendships, and so on and so forth. Identifying client issues is a fairly tricky set of tasks because it challenges life coaches to not take anything at face value.

Identifying Implications

It's one thing to give a piece of advice, it's another to fully map out its implications. This is particularly challenging because it's very easy for many life coaches to fall into the slippery slope of thinking that their job is all about dishing out technical advice. While at some level that is completely true, it misses the bigger picture.

The bigger picture is that you are planting seeds of empowerment in the life of your client.

The person might come to you looking for clothing advice, for example. Your client is going to be going to a job interview and she wants to look really good. She wants to give the right impression. However, to solve that problem, she has to also project herself the right way. To solve that issue, she also has to let go of certain negative mental programming from your childhood. To get to the bottom of that issue, she has to let go of negative feelings about her father or a male figure in her life. Do you see how this works? Do you see how they are all interconnected?

By planting the right seed, the implications are fully mapped out and can lead to not just clear progress, but sustainable progress. In many cases, even a small change in direction can lead to dramatic changes when force is applied. For example, if somebody's going on a fairly straight line at full speed, if you change that trajectory by 2 degrees, they might end up at a completely different place given enough time and enough power.

It's really important for life coaches to get a fairly broad understanding of the implications of their advice. They're not just putting out fires after those fires have broken out.

ProsperWithWayne.com

Instead, their job is to look at the complete forest and see how one action that takes place at a seemingly unrelated area can have a deep and profound impact on another area of that person's life.

Think of your psychology and spiritual make up as a balloon. When you push one side of the balloon, you don't really know which part would swell, but you know another part of the balloon will swell up. That's how a human life works. A lot of the things that you are doing now, a lot of the emotions you're feeling, they were planted there. They are implications of an earlier experience.

The good news is you can reprogram yourself to get out from under the negative programming and adopt positive programming. This is fundamental to the job of a life coach because it's their job to have a fairly clear understanding of the implications of their advice now. It's not just about helping you get that awesome job. It's not just about helping you pick the right clothing, shoes, and accessories. It's all about implications because these implications are what will take your life to the next level or chain you to the status quo.

Coaching Issue-based Solutions

Issue based solutions are all about using very specific hacks to deal with specific issues. Now, this seems pretty straightforward. For example, if somebody has a tough time showing up to work on time, that would require some sort of very targeted response.

This is absolutely true because issue based solutions tend to be quite misleading. They seem very specific, they seem like almost technical, but they do have broad implications. The broad implication is that if you keep repeating these small hacks, they turn into a habit. They change how you think. They change how you view yourself. They change how you see yourself in a wide range of situations.

Issue based solutions are very specific, tightly defined, but can have broad implications. A lot of life coaches say that this is the "bread and butter" of their job. I beg to disagree. While this is where the rubber meets the road, I am of the impression that the more important part of a life coach's job is in the implications of the solutions being recommended.

Progress Tracking

Progress tracking is all about measuring success. There is really no point in seeing a life coach and getting targeted advice and refusing to measure success. It's like going on a diet and not stepping a scale to check how you're doing. It doesn't make any sense.

Progress tracking is very important because it tells the life coach whether the advice is working or not. It also tells the life coach how to mentally and emotionally encourage the client based on where they are in their journey.

It's too easy to look at, for example, weight loss coaching as a simple project of helping a client lose a few pounds. The problem with that is that we tend to fall into the temptation of viewing success primarily as how much weight is lost. The better approach would be to track progress based on where the patient is. For example, if the person uses portion control to minimize their daily caloric intake, the progress should be in how small the portions are and how consistent that person is in eating those smaller portions.

The problem with getting all caught up in "end goals" like pounds lost, money made, members of the opposite sex approach, is that this can easily rob us of our motivation now. For example, if you're just starting out in your business, you obviously are not making millions of dollars every year.

To track your progress and the start up phase based on how much money you made would be flat out sadomasochism. You're just beating yourself up unnecessarily. Why? You're not likely to make money at that early stage. At that early stage, you're just getting the business up, you're networking, you're establishing the right infrastructure, you are discovering the right processes. These are the necessary steps that would pave the way for eventual financial success. To use the "end goal" of financial success as your overarching metric of progress, would simply lead to depression and discouragement.

ProsperWithWayne.com

Scaling Up Success

Life coaches not only help you identify your problem, come up with solutions to those problems and track your progress, they also help you take things to the next level. This is the most exciting part of a life coach's job. The life coach can work with you from point a to point b but the most exciting part is when you go from, for example, making $5,000 a month with your business to $50,000 per month.

Of course, this scaling up process requires a change in mindset, a change in infrastructure, as well as process. Highly competent life coaches would work with a client to go through baby steps and then scaling up those steps for greater and greater levels of mastery until they reach a next level and master that as well.

Go on over to http://www.ProsperWithWayne.com to discover how you can become a professional life coach within just a few weeks!

Chapter 4

How Do Life Coaches Deliver Their Services?

By this point in the book, you should already have a clear idea of what kind of life coaching you'd like to do. Maybe a lot of the life lessons you learned have something to do with success coaching. Alternatively, maybe your life experiences tend to lean more towards doing well with members of the opposite sex so you're thinking about offering dating coaching services.

Whatever the case may be, by this point, you have a fairly good idea of what kind of advice to give and what being a life coach within that particular subject category will require of you. You already know about identifying client issues, paying attention to the implications, progress tracking, offering issue-based solutions, and scaling up their success.

At this point, you will learn about how to deliver those services. Believe it or not, thanks to the internet, the traditional way of coaching people on a face to face, one-to-one basis is just one option. As recently as 20 years ago, it was the only option. There was only one option available if you discount phone-based coaching. The option, of course, is to meet with people on a one-to-one basis and speak to them face to face.

Today, you can provide life coaching services in a wide variety of ways. It's very important to take note of these differences of coaching service delivery because they have a dramatic impact on how much you're going to have to work.

One of the most exciting things about life coaching is that you can provide your services in such a way that you work very little while earning a lot of money. I know this sounds like a pipe dream come true, but it is the reality many life coaches enjoy. Unlike other industries where you are basically stuck working with people on a face to face personal level or standing in front of a live audience, life coaching offers many alternative ways to provide your services.

Just like with the other areas covered by this book, the following discussion is not intended to be a comprehensive "end all be all" description of the different life coaching service delivery methods. I'm sure after a few years or even months under your belt as a life coach, you may even innovate or tweak these delivery methods to come up with your own unique approach.

ProsperWithWayne.com

One-to-One Vs. One-to-Many

Let's just get one thing clear, as a life coach, you are immediately faced with one key decision: are you going to coach on a one-to-one basis or are you going to use a one-to-many approach? This might seem like a fairly straightforward and easy to answer question because, of course, a lot of people would say that the answer is "I'll do both." It's not that easy. The amount of work you have to put in, as well as your preparation, differs tremendously.

If you decide to coach people one-to-one compared to a one-to-many model, one-to-one coaching pays a lot more money, at least superficially. If you're talking about just the amount of dollars you'll make from one particular engagement, it's tempting to assume that one-to-one coaching is where the money is.

One-to-one, of course, means that you are going to set aside a block of your time to talk to somebody either over the phone, Skype, Viber or Whatsapp. The key here is that your client is going to be taking up all your attention for that block of time.

You are going to be walking that person through their issues and then giving that person advice. You would then check up on that person to follow up on their progress, reevaluate the advice you've given, and possibly work with them to optimize results. In most cases, these sessions are not recorded. In most cases, these sessions only have an audience of one: the client.

ProsperWithWayne.com

Another way to provide one-to-one coaching is through email. This can be very tedious because there's a lot of back and forth, there's also a lot of question and answers being bounced around. What makes this particularly inefficient is that it's too easy for either party to overlook an important detail. That important detail might mean the difference between success and failure.

Still, one-to-one consulting is all about you pouring all of your attention to one client. You try to figure out what's going on, you come up with a customized solution, even the follow through and feedback process is customized to the needs and even the personality and expectations of the client.

As you can probably already tell, this highly personalized "high touch" approach is very expensive. A lot of life coaches, especially newbies, get all excited about the prospect of charging a client $400, $500 or even $700 an hour for this type of one to one life coaching. I wish I could say that it's that easy. It isn't. You have to establish a name for yourself to be able to charge that amount of money for one-to-one sessions.

In many cases, while you're still establishing your life coaching practice, you would need to look at the lower end of $100 to $250 for a one-to-one session. It's only after you have established quite a bit of a "grand" in your niche for your coaching services would you be able to attract the clientele who would be ready, willing and eager to pay three figures per coaching hour.

One-to-Many Models

The one-to-many approach may seem like it's small potatoes in the beginning. You might be thinking, if I'm going to be making hundreds of dollars per hour talking to a client, why don't I just do that? Why bother with one-to-many? Well, it may turn out that you would be making more money using a one-to-many model because you charge each person very little money, relatively speaking.

For example, if your normal rate is to coach for $500 an hour, you can charge people $25 or $50 to access your recorded seminars. How does this lead to the big bucks? Well, it's basic economics. The more expensive a service becomes, the lower the demand for that service. You don't have to be a rocket scientist to understand this basic economic principle. It's all about supply and demand.

It's easy to get excited about charging life coaching clients the average rate of $214 an hour, but what's not being said is that those clients come around maybe once or twice every month. For the rest of the time, you're not making money. "Canned" life coaching on the other hand, drastically lowers your coaching rate. Since you recorded the coaching session only once, but play it back many times, you can get away with charging $10, $20, or $50 for access. This makes people less reluctant to try you out.

Your canned webinar videos, when marketed properly, can generate quite a bit of money. Think of it this way, which would you rather have, a hundred clients using your pre-recorded coaching videos, or one $500 per hour client who talks to you once or twice a month? The answer should be a no-brainer. Sure, you're charging less money for each webinar "attendee," but you're making more money overall.

The great thing about canned webinars is that they are great sources of passive income. You only need to record them once, and you can make money from them for the life of the video. For example, if you're going to put up the video and charge for access for several years, you can be making money over those years as people fill out a form and enter their payment information to get access.

Live webinars, on the other hand, is like one-to-one coaching, except you are coaching a crowd. You are speaking to a crowd. What's attractive to this approach is that you can interact with a huge number of people and charge them less money each and still end up making more money than the one-to-one coaching method.

For example, if you're going to be giving a coaching talk on social media marketing ethics, you can charge each attendee $100. If 50 people show up, you make $5,000. Compare this with charging $214 per hour on one-to-one coaching, it doesn't even compare. The best part is that you give the talk only once to make that relatively large amount of money.

Membership-Based Knowledge Base

Another approach you could take is to simply write down all your life hacks, life lessons and important techniques. Maybe you could use a blog form, maybe you could use a formal website form, it doesn't matter. What matters is that you put all that information in some sort of centralized knowledge base that is accessible to all people from all corners of the planet who can access the internet.

They read through your materials and get all excited about your level of expertise. However, once they reach a certain point in the content, they have to sign up for a membership. This membership rebills on a monthly basis. Unless they interrupt the billing cycle, they will automatically get rebilled. Their PayPal accounts will get charged the membership fee month after month after month. If they pay it by credit card, the credit card will be charged that monthly fee every single month unless they stop the rebill.

This is a very powerful coaching method because you work only once. You write down all your thoughts and then that content continues to work for you over a long period of time. This is passive income. You can take your family for a global vacation and not have to worry about paying the rent or paying for your hotel stay because you have all these monthly recurring revenue coming in.

Of course, there is a downside to this. The big disadvantage of this particular model is that you have to promote it adequately. You have to make sure that enough people sign up for your membership site. This requires specialized online marketing skills.

Another key advantage of coaching this way is that you can get away with charging your membership very little money. Maybe you can charge them $5. Most people will not miss $5 a month. In fact, a lot of people would be blind to the $5 being rebilled every single month. As long as there's enough people in your member base, this can produce a very sizable monthly income for you and your family.

Of course, when you charge at a low rate, there is less friction as far as the customer is concerned. They are less likely to object to signing up for your membership site because, hey, it's only $5. Compare this is with a one to one coaching offer where you are coaching somebody at the average rate of $214 an hour.

From the perspective of the consumer, they get the added advantage of getting to go back to your website to review your materials. A Win-Win for both parties involved! Go on over to http://www.ProsperWithWayne.com to discover how you can become a professional life coach within just a few weeks!

Chapter 5

The Coaching Process

Now that you have a clear idea of how to deliver your coaching services and what model you're going to be using, the next step is to get a good idea of the process involved. Make no mistake about it, coaching is a process. It's not some sort of one shot event where somebody talks to you, they say some magic words, you process the information, then you say some magic words to them and the problem magically disappears. It doesn't work that way. There is a process involved and you have to be clear on the different steps of this process so you can deliver a high quality service.

Always remember that bad news travels much faster than good news. If word gets out that you are a lousy coach who is often badly prepared, chances are, you won't get too many coaching opportunities in the near future. The pipeline is just simply going to dry up because the word is out.

By paying attention to the following process steps, you can look more professional, pave the way for better overall service, and open possible opportunities for "upsells." Upsells are sales opportunities where you get your client to pay for more expensive services or buy products and related coaching services. Whatever the case may be, by simply adopting the process I'm going to lay out below, you increase the likelihood that you would be making more money, retaining more of your customers, and ensuring that people walk away with a smile on their faces.

Initial Consultation

The first part of the coaching process is to first get an idea of what the client's problem is. The mere fact that they've contacted you through your website or through social media means **they have a problem they want to solve**. The point of the initial consultation is to determine the parameters of the problem that you are going to be applying your life lessons to. This can be free, paid, or "discounted."

A lot of coaches think that they have to charge for the initial consultation. This really is too bad because if you are going to charge people the moment they go through your coaching business' digital doors, you are putting an unnecessary barrier. They haven't gotten a "taste test" of your service. They don't know whether you know your stuff. They have no idea whether they will get some sort of value from your coaching. This is why a lot of life coaches offer a "free taste" through initial consulting.

The initial consultation is where you blow your client's mind. You demonstrate, in no uncertain terms, your mastery of the specific coaching segment you are offering services under. For example, if you're a dating coach and a very nerdy guy approaches you and tell you that he's a complete flop and a loser with chicks, you can blow that person's mind by telling them stories, giving them actionable hacks that you are sure will work, or otherwise giving them information that they can take action on to produce immediate results.

This increases tremendously the perceived value of your services. In their minds, you're not just some guy blowing smoke. You're not just some self-proclaimed "expert." Instead, every morsel of advice that comes from your lips produces solid value. This can help you establish a solid gold reputation in your field. While that person might not get off the fence and actually pay for your services, you've already done your job. You've already laid the seeds of credibility and authority among the people most likely to talk about you.

Of course, you don't want to shoot yourself in the foot either. You don't want to give away your "secret sauce" during free consultations.

The whole point of free consultations is to give prospective clients a taste of what they're in for if they pay for your consulting or coaching services.

You should give them a teaser. Ideally, you should give them information that you have readily available, but is extremely valuable.

Another approach is to offer a "discounted" service consultation. Using this model, you offer coaching consultation at a ridiculously discounted rate. This reduces the friction, initial objection of your prospective customer. They are more likely to buy if you offer at a discounted rate. You then make up for the discounted rate later once they have signed on to your full service because your full service is priced to compensate you for the discount you offered in the beginning.

Why offer "discounted consultations?" You offer this type of pricing scheme because charging nothing for initial consultation can tarnish your brand. I don't care how established you are in the field, I don't care how many people talk highly of your life coaching service, there is still damage when you put a zero price tag on any kind of service package or product. This is an economic reality.

You basically psychologically price yourself to the bottom end of the cost spectrum. This is a very real danger because if the prospect believes that the initial consultation is free, they are more likely to take a cavalier approach with or have a casual attitude about the value of your services. Since it's free and did not really cost them anything, they can easily discount your advice.

For example, you can advise that lonely person how to meet attractive and interesting people using a specific method you pioneered. You know that that method works. You know this first hand because it works for you like clockwork. However, if the prospect got that advice for absolutely zero cost, then it doesn't really cost them anything to disregard your advice. Do you see how this works?

When you use the discounted pricing method, your prospect at least has some economic sting to worry about. At the very least, they have some sort of investment in trying out your advice. There is some sort of "push" there. There is no such push if the person did not pay for the initial consultation.

Creating a Customized Lesson Plan for Selection of Pre-recorded Modules

Regardless of whether you are offering one-to-one coaching services or one-to-many coaching services, you have to provide a lesson plan. There has to be some sort of sequence in the information you are going to provide your client. This is very easy to do with pre-recorded video modules. You've already recorded these in the past. You just send the set of links to the client and they could access it in sequence.

In a one-to-one context, this is a little bit harder to do because you have to actually pay attention to the specific needs of each client. For example, if you're offering coaching services on how to approach women, some guys are so shy and painfully awkward that they need basic steps like how to say hello or how to smile to strangers, or the basics of body language.

On the other hand, you might be getting a client who has already been around the block. He knows how to talk to women, but he just can't seem to attract the attention of the right woman. These two clients obviously have very different needs. While their overarching concerns tend to overlap, they have very specific needs as far as specific solutions are concerned.

It takes a lot of work for customized, one-to-one coaching because you have to pay attention to this specific set of circumstances surrounding a particular client and coming up with a lesson plan for that client. You then look over your initial consultation notes for the next client and come up with a customized lesson plan for them.

Considering the amount of work involved, it's no surprise that life coaches charge hundreds of dollars per hour for one-to-one consulting. This may seem like a lot of money, but it's actually money well earned because any coach worth his or her salt will customize their lesson plan. Otherwise, they're going to be stuck with "one lesson" clients. Meaning, these clients show up for one coaching session and never show up again.

Client Contact and Coaching

The next step is to contact your client. I know this seems pretty straightforward. In fact, this may seem ridiculously obvious. You might be even thinking, why devote a section to this? Well, believe it or not, given our busy schedules, it's very hard to get a hold of people.

Client contact is a big deal. Even if the person paid hundreds of dollars for your services already, you would still have to chase that person down. Most Americans are busy. Most Americans don't have the luxury of time. There's just so many different things and obligations competing for their time. It's important to set the ground rules for client contact.

You have to remember that you are selling a block of your time. If the client does not make use of that block of time, in most cases, you cannot resell that time to somebody else. This is definitely not going to happen in such short notice. Maybe if the client reserved a time several weeks ahead and notified you at least one week ahead that he or she is not going to make it, you can resell that time.
You need to have a bullet proof contract stipulating that the $300, $400 or $500 fee they paid for one hour of your time is to reserve that time, and if you cannot find a replacement for that time, they forfeit the fee. Most legal jurisdictions recognize such stipulations, but you need to make sure you have it in a bullet proof form. You don't want to use an agreement that is so slippery and so soft that your client can easily walk around it. Make sure that you are compensated for the amount of time you're giving up for that client.

Client Instruction Via Recorded Material

This is much easier. Basically what you do is you create a composite of all the most probable questions your prospects would ask regarding a particular issue. You then record your answers to those questions. You record solutions to their most probable needs.

You then notify your clients to access the recorded materials at their leisure. Once the month is over, they get rebilled for continued access. Their credit card or PayPal account keeps getting rebilled until they put a stop to the rebill process.

Benefits of Live Vs. Recorded Coaching

I know in an earlier chapter I talked about the benefits of "canned" coaching. After all, it's awesome to work only once and get paid many times over tor that work. It's like being a highly paid blogger. You publish a blog post and you make a few pennies that day. But for the life of that blog post, it continues to make money and all these blog post specific earnings pile up.

It's no surprise that in certain niches, bloggers make up to half a million dollars every single year. The funny thing is that they only worked maybe 5 to 10 hours every single week or month. It's not a pipe dream. This actually happens. This is due to passive income using digital assets.

When you record your coaching sessions, you create a passive income digital asset. However, the secret to this is to generate a massive subscriber base to your website. Otherwise, you're not going to be making much money at all.

Go on over to http://www.ProsperWithWayne.com to discover how you can become a professional life coach within just a few weeks!

ProsperWithWayne.com

Chapter 6

How Much Money Can You Make As A Life Coach?

Here comes the good stuff. This is probably the question you have been asking all along as you read this book. I can't say I blame you. As the most famous quote from the Jerry Maguire movie goes: "Show me the money." Make no mistake about it, **you can make quite a lot of money as a life coach.** The best part is that you don't have to work as hard as an active job.

Believe it or not, there are lots of life coaches working all across the United States, making more money than a regular day job and working substantially less. How is this possible? Well, I have already said that the average life coach hourly rate is around $214 per hour. People do pay quite a bit of money for life coaching services.

Now, before you find yourself too excited about that figure, hold on… we will show you many other ways to make much more than that! That amount is based on actual one to one time-based coaching.

You only get paid that figure if you are going to be coaching people directly. You are selling a block of your time to coach that person straight away, and this is called direct income.

Direct income is only one way to prosper as a life coach!

In fact, while the average life coaching rate is $214 per hour, we're dealing with a very skewed statistical distribution. What I mean is that, averages can be quite deceiving. The truth is in the life coaching industry, there are many people who charge thousands of dollars per hour. There are also many people who make no money. You must be trained to coach and trained how to prosper in your own coaching business.

There is no set fee you must charge, there are trained coached charging $100, $250, or even $1,500 per hour. As long as you are getting paid to share your life experiences, there is nothing wrong with charging a rate equal to the value that you bring.

If you are hell bent on only offering direct services, get ready for the frustrating reality. In actuality, you have to be properly trained, able to bring results, and become a recognized authority to become credible enough to command rates of $500, $1000, or even $1500 per hour.

If the reality of that income excites you, then you will be really glad to know the real money is in passive income.

Passive Income

Life coaching can be a tremendous source of passive income. How simple is it to build a recurring monthly income for your family?

You only need to record your coaching sessions and give people access.

Even if you were to charge them a ridiculously low amount of money to access your materials, this can still pave the way for quite a steady stream of income over a long period of time.

Why? Well, you used this "canned" coaching to establish credibility and authority. Once people get a clear idea of what you are talking about and they are confident that you know your stuff, they would be more likely to ask for direct coaching. You can then charge more money by doing that.

In addition to that, if you have established your credibility with them, they are more likely to spread the word about your canned coaching content. People may be drawn to your materials. They would sign up for your website and get rebilled month after month. Eventually, you start building up a community around your canned content.

The best part in all of this is that you don't have to lift a finger to earn that money. You've already put in the work. You already recorded your content, or wrote your materials. For every new person that comes, you don't have to put in the effort.

ProsperWithWayne.com

Do you see how scalable this is?

Do you see how much more preferable this is as far as building your personal brand is concerned to direct coaching?

Now don't get me wrong, there is a space for direct coaching. However, **direct coaching is a premium service.** You only offer that service to people who are willing to pay a pretty penny as for one to one coaching. They have read your books, gone through your website, watched your canned videos, and now they want to go to the next level. They want to pick your brain directly and customized coaching.

In that situation, it makes all the sense in the world, to charge more for your time and services. Why? They want to deal directly with the "guru". At this point, you actually improve the perceived value of your coaching brand by charging a ton of money. It is no surprise that a lot of the big name coaches out there, actually charge thousands of dollars per hour. That is by design.

Let us put it this way. How likely would you be willing to buy a Cartier watch if genuine Cartier watches cost only 20 bucks. Chances are, you won't be as attracted to them as much. Since they're worth thousands of dollars each, you are more likely to buy them because they are a status symbol. Do you see how this works?

A lot of books on life coaching try to pit direct income against passive income. They try to convince you that your best way forward is either direct income only or passive

ProsperWithWayne.com

income only. **My position is that they feed into each other.** By building a solid passive income, as it pays, you lay the groundwork for huge paydays in the future with direct income.

How Do You Make Money With Passive Income?

How long is a ball of string? I don't mean to be flippant, but the truth is, the only limit to passive income as far as life coaching is concerned is your imagination. Anything that you can record once, whether it's text, audio, video, or even pictures, can be a source of supplemental passive income.

This passive material then builds up your brand to such an extent where you become credible enough to pay big bucks through live direct coaching. So what are the supplemental income streams possible? You can write books. There are tons of life coaching books, but you can definitely write it on the Amazon Kindle platform for your sub niche.

Dominate that sub niche. Maybe you specialize in life coaching for recent immigrants to America who are looking to meet members of the opposite sex. In that case, publish tons of books in that sub niche. Speak to all their concerns. While that market may be relatively small, once word gets out through your books, you are sure to corner that market.

Once people learn about you through your books, you start making money through direct coaching, webinars, or a video series. This then brings me to webinars. You can create websites, advertise those, then sign people up to your live events. You can give a live coaching session through this live seminar.

People pay a premium to see you speak live. Why? They can ask questions and interact with you. They can type out their questions and then you can address them through the webinar. You should not make your webinars a one shot deal. You should record them and then charge people to access them.

You can build websites that give access to your videos. By charging a low amount, people get a cheap way to sample your expertise. Once they are convinced that you actually know what you are doing and that you can add value to their lives, you can then "upsell" them to your live webinars, books, specialty reports, or direct one to one coaching. There are just so many ways you can play this game.

Recurring Versus One Time Income

Another factor you need to wrap your mind around is the fact that life coaching can involve recurring income. Sure, a lot of this is small potatoes. We are talking about maybe $5 per member. Every month, they get billed five dollars. But what if in that situation, it may seem like charging $214 an hour makes a lot of sense. I mean $214 is always going to be more than $5.

Now, what if you had more than one member? What if instead of one member, getting rebilled $5 every month, you have 5,000 members being rebilled every month. At that point, it's a no-brainer. The great thing about recurring income is that it can be an appreciating asset if you cultivate it enough by using your books as branding platforms. By using your blog, websites, and books as branding platforms, you can create quite a large recurring income base.

Increase your client volume and you would not have to worry about income because month after month, people pay their five dollar membership. Since you have thousands of members paying like clockwork every single month, this can lead to a massive passive income, and it happens every single month. This is not just a one shot passive income windfall.

Go on over to http://www.ProsperWithWayne.com to discover how you can become a professional life coach within just a few weeks!

Chapter 7

Can You Become A Life Coach Right Now?

By this point, you already have a clear idea of how much life coaches make, the different income models, as well as the different types of life coaching. You also have a fairly clear idea of the different fields of coaching involved and sub-specialties. You might even find yourself very excited about building a passive income empire through life coaching.

Well, here is a little bit of bad news. While you can choose to become a live coach right now, I am telling you it is going to be rough. It's possible to get off the fence and become a life coach and offer your services to the internet. It definitely doesn't cost that much money. I mean, putting up a website doesn't cost much, especially if you are going to be using Wordpress.

The problem is setting up shop right now, with no advanced training or accreditation is going to be very tough. You are going to have quite a steep learning curve in front of you. Why? You are going to have a tough time finding clients, providing a professional level of coaching, and building a multi-tiered coaching income system.

In other words, it is quite challenging to develop a viable life coaching business. It is, after all, a business. It's not a hobby, or some sort of random idea you came across. It requires attention to detail and consistent focus.

Finding clients is especially problematic because nobody

knows you from Adam. You just decided to become a life coach. You feel that you have this very important life lessons that you can share and they may add value to people's lives. Be that as it may, it is going to be very hard to sell your services if people have no way of knowing about those services.

Similarly, without the proper guidance, even if you were to find clients, the kind of coaching experience that they will get might be unprofessional. It might be so substandard that the bad word about your services gets out and you never get another client again.

Finally, coaching right out of the gate with no expert guidance can lead to you building a labor intensive coaching practice. Don't get me wrong. I am not saying that you should not work hard or put in the time or pay your dues. What I am saying is that you have to set up your life coaching the right way. This way, you can maximize the results that you get, for the amount of time, money, and effort that you put in.

Otherwise, you probably spend the vast majority of your time running around in circles. Eventually, you will run out of steam and you end up thinking that it is all a bad idea, and then you quit. As you probably already know, the only way to fail in life is to quit. I don't want you to fail, but unfortunately, that is exactly the kind of road you are on if you don't get expert guidance.

The Bottom Line

The bottom line is, without expert guidance, it's going to

be difficult for you. It will be tough recruiting customers, as well as retaining those clients. Similarly, without expert and proven guidance, it will be very expensive for you. You have to remember that your most important asset is not your money.

Money can be earned again. It can be replaced. Your most precious asset is your time. You would not want to put yourself in a position where you spend months building up your life coaching practice only to find out that you are doing things wrong. Maybe you screwed up on your website, or upon promoting your services, or maybe screwing up your life coaching brand.

Whatever form it takes, screw ups can really set you back in terms of time. While money can easily be replaced or borrowed, time can't. For every minute you spend barking up the wrong tree, you miss out on doing things the right way.

You need expert guidance.

You need a solid framework and experience planning to ensure that your prospective life coaching practice has a high probability of success.

Thankfully, you are in luck. You are reading the book that will give you such expert guidance. I have been there. I make my money **every single day** through life coaching. I know the pitfalls, the mirages, and the real solid sources of and processes for life coaching success.

Go on over to http://www.ProsperWithWayne.com to discover how you can become a professional life coach within just a few weeks!

Chapter 8

Preparing to be a Life Coach (Part 1)

As the old saying goes, if you failed to plan, you're really planning to fail. If you want to be a successful life coach, you need to be properly prepared. I am sure you don't need me to tell you this because you already know this. The problem is the kind of preparation you had in mind is probably no preparation at all.

In too many cases, people who get into the life coaching industry simply jump in with both feet. They hear that it is a fast growing industry, and that the average hourly coaching rate is slightly more than $200 per hour, so they go all in. They jump in with both feet. They are all excited, and then they fail.

Why? They fail to plan properly. Here is how you do it. You have to be both systematic and methodical otherwise you are going to drop the ball. You are either going to end up offering the wrong service or end up failing to attract the right customers. Neither of these situations are good. You have to have a solid framework or game plan otherwise you are only laying the foundations for your ultimate failure.

Conduct A Life Experience Inventory

This is crucial. A lot of would be life coaches think that since they have all these life experiences, they are ready to coach. Since they came up with all these hacks that have made such a big difference in their lives, they are ready to coach. This is absolutely wrong.

The life hacks that you come up with may not be as fully defined as you think. They may be clear in your mind, but the moment you open your mouth or you try writing them down, they might not be as bullet proof as you thought.

The first step is to simply conduct a life experience inventory on yourself.

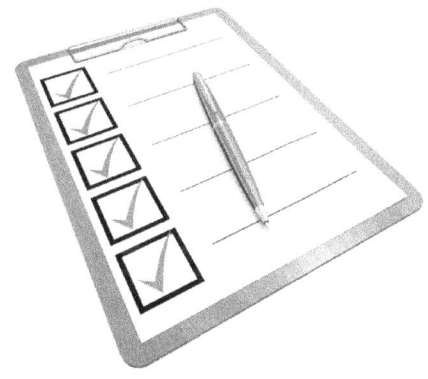

What exactly do you know?
What exactly are your experiences?

What have you been through?

You would be surprised as to how little or how much you know if you ask yourself these questions.
The problem with too many life coaches is that they assume that they know a lot. They assume that their advice is crucial and can be "make or break" advice when it come to success.

However, the moment they actually try to analyze those things, it turns out that they really don't have much of a clue. It may also turn out that their particular "life hack" is so narrowly tailored and so specific to a limited range of circumstances that for all practical purposes are useless to most people.

You don't want to build a life coaching practice with mistaken assumptions regarding the value of the life experience that you have. Sure, they may be very important to you and they may mean a lot as far as your emotions are concerned, but in terms of practical value, they might not be worth much. So, do yourself a big favor. Conduct a life experience inventory.

First, you need to list down your life experiences. Second, list down your hacks. The third step is going to be quite rough. You are going to step into the shoes of people that you are trying to help and honestly assess whether these experiences can actually help them.

If the answer is no, this doesn't mean that you have no future as a life coach, or that you have no business becoming one. All these means is you need to look at the life experiences you already have and reposition them to maximize their value. Maybe you need supplemental information. Cross-refer the life hacks in order to add more value to them.

The truth is, almost any life experience is a valued proposition. They just need to be repositioned or supplemented to maximize the positive impact they would have on people's lives. You need to be completely honest about this process. This is no time to have a sense of denial. As important as you may think your life experiences are, you need to look at them honestly. Otherwise, you might end up building your life coaching business on the wrong foundations and assumptions.

If you notice that there are some discrepancies regarding your knowledge and experience, find supplemental information. Maybe you need to read more about them, or you might want to talk to people who are more experienced in these fields. Whatever the case may be, you need to do some leg work to make sure that your knowledge level is high enough for you to sell it.

Conduct A Counseling Interest Inventory

The next step is to figure out what you would like to counsel people on. Now that you have a clear that you do have life experiences and you know quite a few things, that, in of itself, is not enough for you to start coaching people. You have to first figure out what you are interested in.

Allow me to let you in on a little secret. The more passionate you are about a particular interest category, the better you will be at teaching that interest to other people. **Passion is what drives quality teaching experiences.** You can easily tell if somebody is just going through the motions, or that he or she is just making obligatory points.

When you are passionate about the information you are sharing, you increase the likelihood that the person listening to you will benefit from that information. Why is this important? Well, the more they learn, the more likely they would be to come back to you for more coaching services. They are also more likely to spread the word about your books or tell their friends about your pre-recorded videos. In short, the more passionate you are, the more value you create for your eventual end users.

Conduct a counseling interest inventory. What kind of sub niches in the life coaching industry are most attractive to you? Which interest areas are you more drawn to? Here is a tip. Just because you know a lot more about a particular category doesn't necessarily mean you should coach that category. Why? The passion might not be there. Focus on this happy intersection between passion and knowledge level.

Determining If You Can Deliver On All Your Client's Needs

The next step after you zero-in on a counseling interest category or life coaching sub niche is to determine your probable clients' set of needs. What would they need? What kind of questions are they most likely to ask? Where do these questions lead to? What kind of advice would they be most interested in?

Now that you have laid this all out, cross-reference this with the subjects that you are most passionate about as well as the areas that you are most knowledgeable. Is there a match? If there isn't a match, can you supplement?

Can you get the training you need to be up to speed? Yep. We offer full training for life coach certification – go to

ProsperWithWayne.com

http://www.prosperwithwayne.com and discover how it works.

Remember, it is not about what you need, it's all about your clients' needs. If you are able to meet these, you will have a successful life coaching business. On the other hand, if you can barely satisfy your clients' needs, your business might be mediocre. If you are lacking in any way, then you have no business setting up a life coaching practice. I don't mean to sound harsh, but that is reality.

Determine If You Have The Proper Skills

Now that you have identified the area where you can deliver on your client's needs, as well as the subject area you are most passionate about, the next step is assessing your teaching skills. Like it or not, coaching is all about teaching.

Teaching is when you take an idea in your head and communicate it to another person so they have that idea in their heads as well. It's all about getting the right idea across, getting it absorbed, and most importantly setting in motion a means for the recipient of the idea to put it into action. I mean, let's face it, we can talk until we're blue in the face regarding all sorts of theories and great sounding ideas.

However, they are worthless unless people can actually implement them. For that to happen, you have to get the idea across. This requires patience, proper explanatory skills, and effective teaching. This also involves following up on the person. You can't just give people information, walk them through it, and then leave them alone. It's not going to happen.

Maybe they would implement it once and then fail, and not implement it again. Whatever the case may be, you need to follow up and figure out what they did right, look at space for improvement, and work with them until they achieve the desired results.

Wanting To Teach Is Not Good Enough

I am sorry to be the one to break this to you, but simply getting all excited about teaching, and coaching is not enough. You have to have all the skills required to properly teach. I am not just talking about supplemental information.

For example, you want to teach people to be more productive with their time and maybe you need to learn a few productivity tips. That is just the tip of the iceberg. Information is just one piece of the puzzle. You also have to brush up on proper teaching skills.

Maybe you are not a very patient person, you need to work on that. Probably you are not a very good explainer, then put in some time to get that up to speed. You may not be great at following up, then pay attention to that. I hope this is clear to you. You need to make sure that you have the proper set of skills to properly teach people.

There are lots of very introverted people going into the life coaching industry. They are thinking that since this is computer based and done through the internet that they can make good money simply sharing information. I'm telling you, sharing information is one thing, teaching people is another.

Coaching is teaching. You cannot be in denial about the fact that you may be short on patience, explaining, teaching, or following up skills. No sense of denial is going to do you any good. It's much better looking your shortcomings straight in the eye and do something about them.

The good thing about it is that these are not inborn skills. People you meet who are very patient teachers were not born that way. While there are a few people who have that natural disposition, most good teachers actually learn to be patient. They learn to be great at conveying information and explaining it in terms people would understand.

You can be trained to be a great and prosperous coach!

If they can learn to do that, you can do it too. We are all learning organisms. You just have to have the proper attitude. You have to allow yourself the humility to learn what you need to, so you can be a good life coach. Again, I can't emphasize this enough. Life coaching is teaching.

If you have a low view of teachers, or you think that teaching is not for you, then think twice about life coaching. Chances are, you are being stubborn about not doing something about missing skills. But the moment you open your mind and accept the reality that coaching is teaching, then you can start the process of picking up the supplemental skills you need to become a decent life coach.

Go on over to http://www.ProsperWithWayne.com to discover how you can become a professional life coach within just a few weeks!

ProsperWithWayne.com

Chapter 9

Preparing to be a Life Coach (Part 2)

It's very important to be as methodical and systematic as possible when preparing to be a life coach. This book teaches you how to approach preparing to share your life experiences to others in a very systematic way. Why should you depend on systems? Why shouldn't you do things off the top of your head? Why can't you just do things by the seat of your pants? Well, here's one simple reason: you're less likely to forget stuff.

In your rush to get clients and tell them what you know about life, it's too easy to overlook certain things that can actually mean a great deal, as far as the success or failure of your clients go. You have to pay attention to all the different experiences that you have, and organize them in such a way that they would help your clients. If they don't help, you're not going to have much of a life coaching business left. It's that simple.

You can't assume that just because you are excited about a particular topic, it would be the most relevant to your client. In many cases, they may need a life lesson that you don't really care for. They might benefit more from a life lesson that you find boring or inconsequential. Remember, if you want to be successful as a life coach, your practice has to be about them, not about you. You have to focus on the needs of your clientele. Otherwise, you won't have many clients.

To prepare to be a life coach properly, you need to do the

following:

Create an experience database

At this point, you have written down your experiences. You've also gotten a clear idea as to which areas you need supplementation on. You need to create a database for your life experiences. Try to organize these experiences, and what they mean, based on themes.

Different themes impact various sets of problems. It's important to think in a thematic way. If you are like most people, you have a lot of life experiences. It's too easy to get caught in the details. You may find yourself so busy sorting through all of them, that you forget which experience and lesson would best fit a particular client issue.

Do yourself a big favor and simplify things. Create an experience database, and organize them around themes. You also have to pay attention to the different relevant topics those themes are associated with. This way, when you come across a client with a particular set of problems, you can readily go to your database and whip out life lessons that have a high chance of helping them with their issues.

Create a topic lesson plan

Now that you have a thematically sorted database, the next step is to talk to your client and get an understanding of what exactly they need. Once you have this information, you should create a lesson plan. A lot of life coaches call this a coaching plan or a plan of action; they mean the same thing. You are going to go through this in a methodical way, because the items on this outline are the most relevant to the problems of your client. Your topic lesson plan is going to be episodic. Obviously, you're not going to talk about all the solutions to your client's problems in one sitting. That does not make a lot of sense.

You run the risk of overloading your client with information. Your best bet is to pick the top three themes or the top theme that would best resolve your client's problem. Focus on those and reserve the next theme or topic for the next coaching session. Reducing the number of topics you're going to touch on increase the overall value of your coaching session.

In many cases, a lot of the coaching involves your client talking. Let the client talk; that means they're revealing their heart and soul. When you let them talk, you give them the opportunity to educate you fully regarding the wide range of issues they're grappling with.

This should give you more information, so you can create a topic lesson plan that is extremely relevant to their issues. The more relevant lesson plan, the higher the chances that it would give them the information to achieve a breakthrough.

Create a lesson time plan

One of the most common problems life coaches encounter is they focus so much on how helpful their lesson plan items are. While content is extremely important, timing is just as valuable. You need to lay out the information at the right time. Otherwise, the client is not going to understand, and learn what they need to resolve their issues.

You need to make sure that the topic lesson plans you have planned out for the future follow a logical progression. You cannot start with the end or the middle; you have to start with the beginning. Pay attention to the different experiences you're going to relate, as well as the life lessons you're going to apply to their actual situation.

Check if there's a logical progression; it's usually a good idea to start small and build up over time. You can't just start with a massive concept and expect the client to pick up immediately. You need to spoon feed them at the beginning, and continue to scale things up over time.

The challenge

There is a big challenge with creating a topic lesson plan. In an ideal world, if you follow all my advice above, and you have a very neatly organized experience database, matched by a well-written topic lesson plan being presented according to thoughtful time plan; things will work out properly. Unfortunately, that's not how it is.

In many cases, you may have put in all this time, effort, and energy into a creating a really tight lesson plan and have a great schedule in mind. Then, everything is thrown off track because your client gives you chaotic feedback.

Clients would give feedback in installments. They don't just give them to you in one sitting. In most situations, when you have moved on to another topic, they would look back to the previous topic and talk about issues related to that. It seems that for every two forward steps you take, you take one step backward. They don't follow any logical progression; they don't think the same lines as you.

This is where your patience is going to be tested. Remember, it's all about them; the session is for their benefit and not yours. While you benefit because you're going to be making money off each session, wrap your mind around the fact that this is all about your client. If they want to keep going back, then you need to indulge them. It's going to cost them, but they already now that.

Specializing vs. General Coaching

While focusing on certain coaching sub-niches should give you a fair degree of specialization, this is still somewhat general. It's really important to be clear as to what level of specialization you want to take on. There is such a thing as overspecialization.

For example, if you are going to be coaching people on how to save money, you might think that there are too many life coaches involved in personal finance. You might choose to specialize in graduate student loan issues. This might seem like a good idea on paper, but considering how small that market can be; you might end up with very few clients.

The upside to this is the more specialized you are, the higher your rates can be. Specialization and rates tend to

ProsperWithWayne.com

go in opposite directions. The deeper your specialization, the higher your rates. However, there is an "economic ceiling." You may be so exclusive that there's really not that many people interested in your particular specialty. You have to know where to draw the line.

On the other hand, general coaching ensures that you will have a wider market. The problem is there are also a lot of life coaches shooting for the general coaching market in your sub-niche. Accordingly, you're going to have to deal with a tremendous amount of competition. In the worst case, you end up with a race to the bottom.

For example, if you're in a niche where clients basically think that the body of information you're dealing with is essentially generic, they're not going to pay as much attention to the coach's teaching ability. Instead, they focus on the price; this is exactly what you need to avoid. You can't compete based on price; that is going to be a losing proposition for you. The antidote to this is specialization, but you can't overdo it. Otherwise, you cut yourself out of your market.

Creating a system that can handle individualized coaching

The best way to pair individualized coaching with prerecorded coaching is to create a database of written materials that you can easily access. Once you have this database, you can just mix and match the lessons that you've handled in the past to meet your current client's needs. You will be able to recycle old work, if done properly. At the same time, you earn a much higher rate because you're offering this information on a one-to-one basis. Think of this as a happy marriage or middle ground between prerecorded or canned coaching and live, highly customized, and personalized coaching services.

Go on over to http://www.ProsperWithWayne.com to discover how you can become a professional life coach within just a few weeks!

Chapter 10

Trial And Error Can Doom Your Life Coach Career

What could go wrong if you just go out there and not get appropriate training as a life coach? What can possibly happen if you do not have the proper accreditation? Well, the short answer is: everything!

First, nobody wants to be your guinea pig. If people can tell that you are just trying your hand at life coaching, and you don't really have formal training or accreditation, people will steer clear of you. It's obvious that you're going to be testing your own improvised teaching systems on them, and they might not benefit all that much from what you have to say. People don't like to waste their time. If they can tell that you're basically learning at their expense, they would not want to try your services. Even if you were to charge them a very low amount of money, people wouldn't want the hassle.

Another thing that could go wrong is looming competition. You have to understand that the vast majority of life coaches out there are not formally trained, nor did they go through some structured accreditation system. They are mostly self-taught. They have developed a local clientele, and branched out to global market thanks to the internet. These people are your competition.

With our professional life coaching certification program you will be light years ahead of those other people, and you will have a step by step plan to succeed as a six-figure life coach! Go now to http://www.ProsperWithWayne.com

to discover more.

If you are going to go through your life coach career on a trial-and-error basis, you're going to have to live with the fact that you have all this competition. They don't have accreditation like you; they are self- taught, and they are doing things by the seat of their pants. This leads to a race to the bottom. You have to cut your rates time and again just to attract clients and hang onto them.

It's also worth noting that if you fail to specialize, you will eventually get caught by surprise by your competition. It's that basic. The market for life coaching is fast evolving. People are beginning to prefer more specialized service providers. It's only a matter of time before the days of "general practitioner" life coaches are a thing of the past. This is a natural progression.

When medicine first became a profession in the US, most physicians were general practitioners. However, as the science of medicine continued to evolve, most patients' focus turned to specialization. Life coaching is no different. People are beginning to expect and demand specialization. You don't want to get caught by surprise by this threat. You might end up waking up to the fact that nobody wants your services because you're not specialized enough.

Another issue you need to be on the lookout for is that bad online reviews travel faster than good news. In many cases, people couldn't care about the fact you made somebody happy, or you changed someone's life for the good. They couldn't care less about that good news.

Instead, they pay attention to that one time when you gave terrible advice, and somebody felt ripped off by you. Unfortunately, without proper training, it's too easy to get bad online service reviews.

So what is the worst that can happen?

Even if you drop the ball, you might be thinking that it's not that bad. A few bad reviews here and there couldn't kill you, right? Think again. You have to understand that in this industry, given its level of competition, it's very difficult to get a career reboot as a coach if you screw up. Once people hear that you screwed up, you can call it a day. It's game over for you.

Why? There are so many life coaches out there to choose from. Why should they waste their time and money with you? You're damaged goods to them. You see how this works? Sadly, it's not just about the quality of your coaching services.

Even if you were to provide really good coaching services, your bad marketing decisions in the past can bankrupt you. Maybe you said the wrong thing or you represented yourself a certain way. Whatever the case may be; you left a bad taste in the mouths of your potential clients, and these marketing decisions can come to haunt you. Not just once, but again, and again, and again.

This all traces back to the fact that self-styles or unaccredited coaches are a dime a dozen. Anybody can call themselves a life coach. There are no state regulatory system you have to go through, no bar exam, or medical boards to pass. You just have to put up a website, post a nice picture of yourself with the designation life coach, and you're in business. This is how many fly-by-night and shady life coaches operate. There are also respectable and decent life coaches that do the same thing. They just put up a website and offer coaching services.

The problem here is one of perception. Consumers really have no way of knowing which coaches are trustworthy. There are too many unaccredited coaches out there that the market is wising up. It only takes one nightmare story for prospective clients to get the hint. They don't want to be separated from their hard-earned dollars. They don't want to feel they got ripped off. Unfortunately, this is precisely what's happening due to the shenanigans of too many unaccredited and undisciplined life coaches out there. Go on over to http://www.ProsperWithWayne.com to discover how you can become a professional life coach within just a few weeks!

Chapter 11

The Key To Life Coach Success: Proper Accreditation

Considering all the things that could go wrong, and the hard reality of the life coaching industry, you need a competitive edge. You need to have something that will make you stand above your competition. As I've mentioned previously, the vast majority of life coaches out there are really unaccredited. They're not part of any organization; they did not go through a structured process to become life coaches. They just put up a website, and started recruiting clients.

Don't get me wrong. A large number of people who do things this way are decent. They don't burn or defraud anybody. The problem is it only takes one bad apple to spoil it for everybody else, and that's precisely what's happening in the global life coaching industry.

You need some form of protection against the increasing skepticism the public has about life coaches. This is why proper accreditation is so powerful. It's not just a piece of paper or a badge you put on your website; it's something more. It lets the clients know that you offer the following:

Systems-based approach

Proper accreditation means that you use a system to provide your services. You're not just saying things off the top of your head. You're not making up stuff as you go. Instead, you have a system in place that properly categorize your life lessons. You also have a systematic approach to listening to your clients to get a clear idea of their issues. You use a systematic way to tie your life experiences to their issues. This increases the likelihood of three things.

First, it increases the chances that they would understand you clearly. Second, it boosts their confidence, and they are able to take action on your suggestions. Third, you provide coaching in a way that any actions done by your clients can be plugged into a success tracking system. Systems work; it ensures that no important piece of information falls between the cracks.

Proper accreditation involves standardization

When you get accredited, or go through a structured accreditation process, you can bet that all the material you'll be exposed to is standardized. You're not left guessing; you're not left to your own devices to come up with your information. Instead, you work from the same basic framework, and you plug in your individual life lessons. This common framework enables you to communicate with your clients in a way that they can take your specialization and other professional information and compare you with other providers.

Standardization is crucial because you don't want to provide services in a very erratic way. You don't want to show up one day, and just knock the ball out of the park by the high quality of your teaching. The next day you show up in a foul mood, and the student can barely get anything useful out of you. With proper standardization, you won't have that variation in quality. Everything will be covered the right way using the same set of evidence and facts.

Accreditation shifts your attention to the results

One common weakness of many life coaches is they get all caught up in the process of coaching. This is easy to understand. For example, when was the last time you explained something to somebody? I am sure that at some point in the past, you were explaining something that was personally exciting to you. You get so caught up in the excitement that you fail to realize that the people didn't really understand what you're trying to get across.

Results oriented focus shifts your attention to the results. You have to speak clearly, so that the information you're trying to get across is absorbed properly. This helps ensure that the person is emotionally motivated enough to take action on the information you provided. When they do this, they start producing results. Proper accreditation system focuses on increasing the likelihood of certain results happening. It doesn't guarantee it, but it increases the probability that you will get your desired results.

Marketing guidance is crucial

Accreditation provided by competent online and offline institutions is also going to give you important guidance, as far as marketing and business in general go. You would at least get a framework for marketing your life coaching business. You would get a clue as to which traffic sources to work on first, how to scale up your traffic flows, and as well as maximizing the marketing value of your website's content. These all go together.

The same applies to business guidance. Life coaching is a business. You might be having a lot of fun or passionate about the topics, but believe me; it's a business. You have to run it like one. Accreditation systems are geared towards people who want to run their life coaching practice as a business. You can pick up some important productivity and organizational tips.

The bottom line

It's simple. When you get accredited, you gain a competitive advantage. You're not just some random person who started calling themselves "life coach," those people are a dime a dozen. Instead, you have an accreditation you can use to tell your website visitors that you stand apart from the competition. You went through the process, paid your dues, and put in the time. As a result, you have this accreditation.

This tells the client that you have a system of teaching. Your system involves materials and processes that are standardized. It also lets the clients know that results matter to you. Putting all these together, you would be foolish not to get accredited. Accreditation may not make your business a customer magnet overnight, but it gives you a competitive advantage over a vast majority of life coaches out there.

When you sign-up with us to become a professional life coach, you will be accredited through IACCC – International Association of Coaches Counselors and Consultants. You will have complete training and support that you need to reach your dreams and goals as a coach.

Go on over to http://www.ProsperWithWayne.com to discover how you can become a professional life coach within just a few weeks!

Chapter 12

Getting The Word Out About Your Life Coaching Practice

This chapter assumes that you have set up your life coaching website. The next step is to let the world know. If people haven't heard of your coaching services, then you would not get clients. If you don't get clients, you don't make money. You need to be able to get out the word. You can either pay for it, or you use free online marketing methods.

Sadly, there is no such thing as free

The bad news is that there's no such thing as free online traffic. Why? You have to remember that to get free online traffic, you have to spend time. If you don't have any money that's ok, you just have to spend time creating accounts and content, engaging people, and eventually driving them to your website. This may not be costing you money, but this is definitely costing you time. Since time is money, it follows that you are spending money in the form of opportunity costs.

What are opportunity costs? Imagine if you were doing something for $5 an hour, when you could have been doing something that's worth $400 an hour. Your opportunity cost in this situation is $395 per hour. Opportunity costs are higher-value activities that you could have otherwise engaged in. Remember, you can only do one thing at a time.

With that said, what are the free online marketing methods

available? You can do any one or a combination of any of the following activities. You can post on forums and advertise your website through your signature line. You can participate in discussions and drop your line in context as part of the discussion.

You can also try driving free traffic through blog commenting. Believe me, this works. The secret sauce? You have to find the right blogs. In short, look for niche specific, categories, or topic-specific blogs to comment on.

Social media can be a tremendous source of traffic. You just create social media accounts and share your content on those platforms. Eventually, you will be able to get a nice stream of traffic from social media.

Guest posting is also a great way to get free traffic. You look for blogs that cater to the same life coach sub-niche topics as you, and you contribute a blog post. This is a good way to reach out to other client bases to your audience who may be reading certain blogs in your niche. You definitely get an opportunity to position yourself as an expert.

Finally, you can submit expert articles to big media brands like Forbes and others. This is not a slam dunk. You have to produce high-quality articles. Otherwise, your submitted material would not get published.

The big disadvantage with taking the free route is they often take a long time. In many cases, it may be so long and drawn out that you're better off just paying for traffic.

ProsperWithWayne.com

Paid online marketing methods

Paid online marketing is really all about buying traffic. You can buy traffic in the form of pay-per-click. The most prominent example of this is Google's AdWords system. You can also buy advertising directly from high-traffic websites. You can rent space in the emails sent by email marketers in your life coaching niche. Finally, you can invest in social media ads.

The big advantage of paying for traffic is you get it right away. It's like turning on a faucet, and traffic comes out. The downside is that it can get very expensive immediately. This is especially true if you don't know what you're doing. If you don't know how to fine-tune your campaign, you might want to hold off spending money on online advertising. Why? It would lead to the ridiculous situation of throwing good money after bad.

Key tips for life coaching success

If you really want to be successful with your fledgling life coaching business, pay attention. Here are some key tips to maximize the chances of you succeeding with your life coaching venture.

Highlight your accreditation

The first thing you need to do is to highlight the fact that you are accredited. This gives you instant credibility. People don't have to poke and ask around to figure out whether they are going to respect you or not.

When you show your accreditation, people instantly respect you. After all, you went through that process while most other life coaches simply didn't bother.

Put up a professional website

It's important to make sure that you have a professional online presence. Unfortunately, simply creating a nice-looking front page is not going to cut it. You have to use a professional website designer to put together a website that can become your graphical brand. When people talk about your service, they should be able to think back on that well-crafted advertising graphic highlighting your company's total value proposition.

Another reason why you should seriously consider putting up a professionally designed website is the fact that this is going to be the home of all your online branding efforts. You need to direct all the customer engagements you find

ProsperWithWayne.com

yourself in towards your home page. All that effort must flow towards building up the brand value and equity of your professional website.

This leads to the next tip for success: build a solid online brand. You have to focus on creating a brand for yourself. You can't just lose yourself in the empty details of how to drive more traffic. Your brand is like a battery. You may be pumping a lot of marketing into it now, but once you're no longer actively marketing your product; you may have established such a solid brand that this continues to attract customers.

Here at IACCC **we can provide you a professional life coaching website** when you make the great decision to become certified with our association.

Create an account on all social media platforms

To increase your chances of success, make sure that you make use of all the resources made available to you. Social media platforms can definitely help you with this. You only need to share with the right people. If these people are very influential, and if they share your content, even more people will see your content. It is no surprise that internet trends and viral content break out all over the internet even though they were originally distributed to a small group of people. It doesn't matter how big your social circle is. As long as you are connected to enough influential people, your message will go out.

Blog your expertise

In addition to having a service website that is professionally done, you should also put up a blog. Your blog is not wasted space. It actually provides you with a tremendous amount of opportunities to talk about your expertise. The more you talk about your expertise; the more people will hear about it. And it's more likely that they would order services from you.

The key part of effective blogging is to blog about the success stories involving your product or service. This is called social proof. Prospective customers will remain on the fence until they get a third party corroboration for the quality of the products or services you are offering.

Client testimonials can go a long way. You've probably seen a lot of these and feel that these leave nothing to be desired. But, be that as it may, when you feature testimonials, people can't help but be automatically drawn. When people share something about their experiences, people are more likely to listen. Don't let that opportunity go to waste.

Issue press releases

It's very important to create a newsworthy angle to your business. Once you have this angle finely crafted, you should pick the best online press release distribution company. There is a handful of them, but after experimentation with each, you can find the best fit for your needs.

Don't forget to network

ProsperWithWayne.com

There's no shortage of life coaching conventions taking place all across the year in the US and elsewhere. Take advantage of this. When you rub shoulders with other accredited coaches, you might stumble upon important solutions to problems that have been holding you back. Don't be afraid to network.

Keep in mind that you don't know everything. The people that you meet have different experiences from you. These differences are a blessing; they enable you to look at an issue from more than one perspective. You should also be able to get inside information on how to be more patient, and how to explain concepts better.

Don't overlook your existing client base

Another way you can spread the word about your life coaching business is simply to ask your existing clients if they can refer you. In exchange for this kindness, you may want to give discounts to your clients if they hook you up with volume clients or large corporations.

Build passive income streams based on your active coaching

I need you to think of a big picture here. You should not just be getting into life coaching because you've got nothing better to do. You shouldn't be doing it out of desperation. Instead, you should be systematic about the income you're going to generate from life coaching. You should look into setting aside some of that money so you can produce webinars, members only areas, books, and audio books.

ProsperWithWayne.com

Once you start making money from these passive income assets, you can roll over the money to other activities. The point here is that you can build a passive income stream without a lot of money. You can just offer coaching services and build up capital to start creating coaching systems that are self-sustaining.

Go on over to http://www.ProsperWithWayne.com to discover how you can become a professional life coach within just a few weeks!

Conclusion

Life coaching is a tremendous industry. Where else can you get paid to talk about stuff you are excited about?

You can literally have a six-figure income as a coach in just months! One of our coaches loves to brag how they clear $10,000 months with a simple I-Phone and a $2.00 notebook from Staples!

When you sign-up for our life coach certification program you will receove not only to tools to coach, but also the tools to succeed financially as well.

As soon as you complete the certification process, which is done by computer in the convenience of your home or office, you will personally have a coaching session with myself, to discuss your dreams and goals as a coach. This power strategy session will jump start your career and success!

Also, you will receive our private masterclass not available for sale anywhere else, at any price, absolutely free - **"How To Earn Your First $10,000 In Life Coaching!"** This video teaching resource has created an amazing lifestyle for so many of our clients!

By reading this book and implementing its tips, you increase your likelihood of success. Don't take any of these tips lightly. They are a product of many years of experimentation, trial-and-error, and paying one's dues.

Are you ready to finally live the life you were created to

ProsperWithWayne.com

live?

Are you ready for a six-figure or even a seven-figure (yes there a million dollar paydays in the business) lifestyle?

I invite you to the very rewarding industry that has truly change dmy life, and will change yours as well.

Is it for you?

Let's get you some information and see – in fact, lets get on the phone and chat!

There is no charge for a call – in that we will discuss your dreams and answer any questions that you may have about being a professional life coach with IACCC. We'll need about 25-30 minutes together, and as always there is never any obligation.

ProsperWithWayne.com

Go to http://prosperwithwayne.com/me-a-life-coach-how-does-life-coach-certification-work/
and once you read over the page click on the button to set up a time to connect!

A few questions for you…

How would your life change with a real $100,000 per year, or more, income from home?

What would you do different than now?

Are you ready for more?

You deserve all of the success and we have the ticket for you!

ProsperWithWayne.com

I look forward to speaking with you soon!

 Wayne Sutton Founder & President
IACCCC & ProsperWithWayne.com

Go now to:

http://prosperwithwayne.com/me-a-life-coach-how-does-life-coach-certification-work/

www.ingramcontent.com/pod-product-compliance
Lightning Source LLC
Chambersburg PA
CBHW060402190526
45169CB00002B/715